"Children and adults will love these gentle, empowering books. The Learning to Get Along series is a powerful tool for teaching children essential social skills such as empathy, respect, cooperation, and kindness. This straightforward and insightful series helps children visualize how their appropriate behavior positively impacts themselves and others. I heartily recommend this as a solid, classic resource for teaching affective skills to young children."

—Dr. Stephen R. Covey, Author, *The 7 Habits of Highly Effective People*

Join In and Play

Cheri J. Meiners, M.Ed.

Illustrated by Meredith Johnson

Library of Congress Cataloging-in-Publication Data

Meiners, Cheri J., 1957–
Join in and play / Cheri J. Meiners ; illustrations by Meredith Johnson.
p. cm. — (Learning to get along)
Summary: Simple text discusses how to develop the skills to make friends and play with others. Includes role-playing activities.
ISBN 1-57542-249-2
1. Play—Juvenile literature. 2. Social skills—Juvenile literature. 3. Friendship—Juvenile literature.
[1. Play. 2. Social skills. 3. Friendship.] I. Johnson, Meredith, ill. II. Title.
GV1203.M37 2004
790—dc22

200301987

Cover and interior design by Marieka Heinlen
Edited by Marjorie Lisovskis

10 9 8 7 6 5 4 3 2 1
Printed in Hong Kong

Free Spirit Publishing Inc.
217 Fifth Avenue North, Suite 200
Minneapolis, MN 55401-1299
(612) 338-2068
help4kids@freespirit.com
www.freespirit.com

Free Spirit Publishing is a member of the Green Press Initiative, and we're committed to printing our books on recycled paper containing a minimum of 30% post-consumer waste (PCW). For every ton of books printed on 30% PCW recycled paper, we save 5.1 trees, 2,100 gallons of water, 114 gallons of oil, 18 pounds of air pollution, 1,230 kilowatt hours of energy, and .9 cubic yards of landfill space. At Free Spirit it's our goal to nurture not only young people, but nature too!

Dedication

To the princess of charm,
who bubbles with laughter
and affection,
Andrea Rose

Acknowledgments

I wish to thank Meredith Johnson for her beautiful illustrations. I also thank Judy Galbraith and all those at Free Spirit who believed in this series. Special thanks go to Marieka Heinlen for the lovely design and to Margie Lisovskis who, as editor, has contributed her wonderful expertise and creativity. Finally, I am grateful to Mary Jane Weiss, Ph.D., whose insight, skill, and caring have done much to advance the field of teaching social skills.

Magic Tricks

I like to play.

I can do lots of things alone.

Sometimes, I'd rather play with a friend.

When I see someone I'd like to play with,
I can walk up and smile as I say hello.

The person might be looking for a friend, too.

I can tell something about me
or ask a question.

I can listen.

I can answer in a nice way.

Sometimes my friend invites me to play along.

I can also ask to play.

I might think of a way to join in.

When I ask to join in,
people might say no.

I can ask again later.

Or I can look for a different friend to play with me.

If I need help joining in
I can ask a grown-up.

Can I play, too?

I can invite someone to play with me.

I can tell my ideas
and listen to other ideas, too.

When we share ideas, we are cooperating.

I can play with more than one friend.

My friends can, too.

I want everyone to get along.

Sometimes I lose a game,
or get picked last,
or don't get a turn.

I can still have fun.

And things might go better next time.

When things don't go well for someone else, I can say something kind.

A person may do something that I don't think is fair.

I can say how I feel.

If I also listen to how the other person feels, we may solve our problem.

Okay. I'm almost done.

I can play fair and follow the rules.
I can listen and speak kindly.
I can share and wait my turn.

I can show respect.

When I join in and play,
I can make friends by being a good friend.

Ways to Reinforce the Ideas in *Join In and Play*

As you read each page spread, ask children:

- What's happening in this picture?

Here are additional questions you might discuss:

Page 1

- What are some things you like to play when you're by yourself?

Pages 2–11

- What are some things you like to do with a friend?
- When you want to join in and play with someone, what can you do? *(Discuss ideas like saying hello; watching for a while to show interest and to figure out a way to join in; asking a question or starting a conversation; asking to play; and suggesting a way to join in. For example, on page 11, the girl might offer to turn the rope so the boy could jump.)*
- If you are playing and see someone who might like to join you, what can you do? What can you say?

Pages 12–13

- Is it ever okay to say no when someone wants to play with you? When are some times people might say no? What are some nice ways to say no?
- If you ask to join in and someone says no, what can you do?
- Do you think these children could have found a way to say yes? What could they have done?

Pages 14–15

- When might you need help joining in?
- Who are some grown-ups who can help you?

Pages 16–21

- Have you ever invited someone to play? What did you say?
- Why is it fun to play games with other people?
- What does it mean to cooperate? How are these children cooperating?
- What are some ways you cooperate when you play?

Pages 22–23

- How does this boy feel? What do you think he will do?
- Have you ever been sad because someone wouldn't play with you? What did you do?

Pages 24–27

- What problem do these children have? How did the children solve their problem?
- What can you do when you feel someone isn't being fair to you?

Pages 28–29

- What are these children doing to get along?
- What is respect? How does taking turns (following rules, playing fair) show respect? *(You might explain respect by saying, "When you show respect to people, you show that you think they are important.")*

Pages 30–31

- How are these children being good friends?
- Think about children you play with. How do they show that they are good friends?
- What can you do to be a good friend?

Join In and Play teaches beginning skills children can use to join and welcome others in play. Playing cooperatively is a complex activity for young children, involving a mix of skills and understandings. Observation helps children be aware of other people's actions, feelings, and needs. Cooperation begins when children are able to both assert themselves appropriately and develop a welcoming attitude toward others. Being a good sport teaches others to reciprocate. Playing fair involves several skills: following game rules, taking turns, sharing, listening, expressing feelings, speaking with kindness, cooperating, compromising, and solving problems.

Here are three guidelines you can use to support children as they develop skills for playing with others:

1. Watch and listen.

2. Ask and invite.

3. Play fair.

"Joining In" Games

Read this book often with your child or group of children. Once children are familiar with the book, refer to it when teachable moments arise involving both positive behavior and problems related to playing together. In addition, use the following activities to reinforce children's understanding of how to join together and play (adapting them as needed for use with a single child).

"Play" Practice

Preparation: Collect some toys and games to be used as props. On index cards, write prompts similar to the following. Place the cards in a bag.

Sample Prompts:

- Ask, "May I play with you?"
- Ask, "What are you doing?"
- Ask, "Can I have a turn?"
- Say, "That looks like fun."
- Ask, "Can I use that when you're done?"
- Ask, "Do you want a turn?"
- Ask, "Would you like to play with this now?"
- Ask, "What do you want to play?"
- Say, "You can go first."
- Ask, "Do you want to play with me?"

After a child draws a card, read or have the child read it aloud. Invite the child to choose a toy, approach a nearby child, and say what is on the card. The two children can then briefly act out a scene of joining in to play. Encourage the exchanges and play to continue for a short time, prompting and assisting as needed. The child who was approached can then draw the next card and approach a different child. Continue play until each child has had a turn drawing a card.

What Would You Do?

Present a play-related problem situation to children and discuss possible solutions with the whole group. Then break children into small groups of two to four. Tell each group to decide on one way to help solve the problem. Monitor how the groups are doing and help guide their discussions as needed. Allow groups three or four minutes to talk about the problem. Then have the small groups take turns telling their ideas to the whole group. Use the following examples of problems that occur during play (or make up your own).

Examples: Someone called someone else a mean name, tried to be the boss of the game, pushed another person who was in line for the slide, took something someone else was using, wanted to follow different game rules, left in the middle of a game.

Possible Solutions: Let children know that there are several appropriate responses. Among other choices, these might include: telling the person how you feel, ignoring what someone did, talking to an adult, thinking of a way to be friendly next time you see the person, calmly reminding the person of the rule, and smiling. Remind children that it is always best to "treat others as you want to be treated," and not to respond unkindly in return.

I Have Lots of Friends

Have children place chairs in a circle, with one chair too few. Invite one child to stand in the center of the circle while the others sit. Ask the standing child to think of a favorite activity (for example, playing tag at recess). Then have the child call out, "I have lots of friends who like to play tag at recess." Those who like to play tag jump up and join the child in the middle. Then all scramble for a new seat, and the one left standing is the next caller. If needed, help callers come up with other play ideas (for example, building towers, dressing up, swings, card games). During or after the game, discuss the activities the children mentioned, and talk about which children liked each activity. Help children recognize that there are many friends to invite and ask to play, and discuss ways they might form groups and play together.

"We Are Friends" Mural

Materials: Slips of paper with children's names written on them; drawing paper, crayons or markers, pencils or pens

Place the name slips in a bag or other container. Have each child draw the name of another child in the group. (If your group has an uneven number of children, draw the name of a child who will draw two names from the container.) Say: "We are going to make a mural that shows how we can play with different friends. On your paper, draw a picture of yourself playing with the friend whose name you drew." When children are done drawing, have them write (or dictate for you to write) a description of what they are doing with their friends in their pictures. The pictures may depict actual or imagined play. Each child will be featured in two pictures; one drawn by the child and one by a classmate. Display the pictures as a mural on the bulletin board or along a wall. Label the mural "We Are Friends."

Other Suggestions for Helping Children Join In and Play

Encourage smiles and laughter. Humor is an important part of children's healthy social and emotional growth. Encourage and join in riddle- and joke-telling, silly dress-ups, exaggerated expressions and voices. Enjoy laughing together at appropriate times. Children who develop humor also develop assertiveness and empathy for others—both important traits in making friends. Children who can laugh at situations and have fun are sought out by other children. Potential conflicts can also be averted at times with humor or a smile.

Encourage and reinforce inclusive play. Encourage your child or group to be kind to all children; especially those who are new or who are looking for a friend. Applaud friendliness, taking turns willingly, and sporting attitudes. At home, provide a welcome atmosphere for your child to play with friends; be available to guide children to play cooperatively. At school, encourage children to welcome newcomers, to initiate play with different friends as well as with familiar ones, and to be creative in finding ways to invite and include others in play.

More titles in Free Spirit's Learning to Get Along® series:

Our Learning to Get Along® series by Cheri J. Meiners, M.Ed., helps children learn, understand, and practice basic social and emotional skills. Real-life situations, lots of diversity, and concrete examples make these read-aloud books appropriate for childcare settings, schools, and the home. Each book: $10.95, 40 pp., color illust., S/C, 9" x 9", ages 4–8.

ACCEPT AND VALUE EACH PERSON
Introduces diversity and related concepts: respecting differences, being inclusive, and appreciating people just the way they are.

REACH OUT AND GIVE
Begins with the concept of gratitude; shows children contributing to their community in simple yet meaningful ways.

TALK AND WORK IT OUT
Peaceful conflict resolution is simplified so children can learn to calm down, state the problem, listen, and think of and try solutions.

UNDERSTAND AND CARE
Builds empathy in children; guides them to show they care by listening to others and respecting their feelings.

SHARE AND TAKE TURNS
Gives reasons to share; describes four ways to share; points out that children can also share their knowledge, creativity, and time

WHEN I FEEL AFRAID
Helps children understand their fears; teaches simple coping skills; encourages children to talk with trusted adults about their fears.

BE POLITE AND KIND
Introduces children to good manners and gracious behavior including saying "Please," "Thank you," "Excuse me," and "I'm sorry."

LISTEN AND LEARN
Introduces and explains what listening means, why it's important to listen, and how to listen well.

KNOW AND FOLLOW RULES
Shows children that following rules can help us stay safe, learn, be fair, get along, and instill a positive sense of pride.

RESPECT AND TAKE CARE OF THINGS
Children learn to put things where they belong and ask permission to use things. Teaches simple environmental awareness.

TRY AND STICK WITH IT
Introduces children to flexibilty, stick-to-it-iveness (perseverance), and the benefits of trying something new.

To place an order or to request a free catalog of Self-Help for Kids® *and* Self-Help for Teens® *materials, please write, call, email, or visit our Web site:*

Free Spirit Publishing Inc.
217 Fifth Avenue North • Suite 200 • Minneapolis, MN 55401 • toll-free 800.735.7323 • local 612.338.2068
fax 612.337.5050 • help4kids@freespirit.com • www.freespirit.com